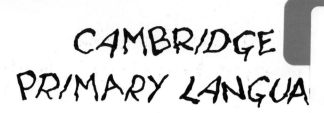

G000139710

Contents

(Red numbers show activity pages)

Me

Carefully read all of Krisha's writing on page 3.

1 Write about yourself in the same way.
Use Krisha's **headings** and words to help you.

2 Think of and write another **heading**.
Under it write something else about yourself.

3 Draw and colour a picture of yourself.

Me

Myself

My name is Krisha. I am seven years old.
I have brown straight hair. My eyes are
brown. Today I am wearing a red
blouse and a grey skirt.

My family

I live with my mother and father in
York. I have two brothers. They are
Henry who is nine and Brian who
is six.

My favourite things

My favourite things are my pets. I have a
rabbit and a guinea-pig. The rabbit is
called Silky. The guinea-pig is called
Gilbert.

David's house

Carefully read the writing on page 5.

1 Use the writing to help you draw the front of David's house.
Start by drawing the shape about this size.

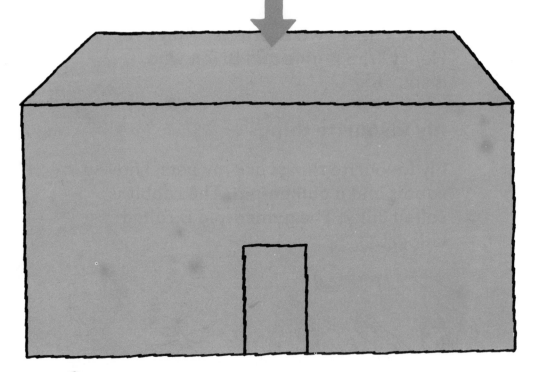

2 Write two ways in which David's home is **different** from yours.

3 Write two ways in which David's home is **the same** as yours.

David's house

The door is in the middle of the front of the house.
There is a round window in the top half of the door.
At each side of the door there is a large square window.
Above the door is a smaller square window. On each
side of this there is another window which looks just
the same. The chimney is at the top of the roof.
It is in the middle. It has a TV aerial.

If you stood looking at the front of David's
house you would see a gate on the right side and
a tree on the left.

Lee's friends

 Search page 7 and use the **headings** to find out.

1 Which friend has Lee known for five years?

2 Which friend lives next door to Lee?

3 Where did Lee first meet Azmat?

4 What summer game do the friends play at school?

5 Where do the friends play when they are not at school?

6 How many children go swimming altogether?

7 What do you and your friends like doing when you are not at school?

Lee's friends

My friends

My name is Lee. I have two good friends.
Their names are Tim and Azmat. I have known
Tim for five years. He lives next door to me.
I first met Azmat at school. That was
two years ago.

At school

When I am at school I often play with my friends.
In the winter we play football. In the summer we
usually play rounders.

Out of school

When I am not at school I play in the park with
Tim and Azmat. Sometimes the three of
us go swimming. Azmat's two young
sisters go with us.

My senses

Search page 9 to find out.

1 How many parts of the body are named on page 9? Write a **list** of them.

2 Write these sentences and put in the missing senses.

I use my sense of_____when I see a cat.
I use my sense of_____when I touch wood.
When I eat chocolate I use my sense of_____.

3 How many senses are written about on page 9?

4 Draw this picture. Write a label for each sense.

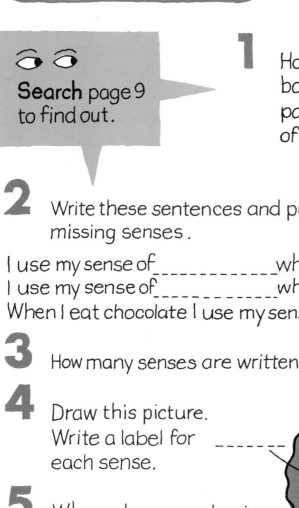

5 Where does your brain get information from?

6 Finish these:

A sight I like is_____.
A sound I hate is_____.
A smell I like is_____.
A taste I hate is_____.
I like to touch_____.

My senses

I see with my eyes. I hear with my ears. I smell
with my nose. I taste with my tongue. I use my fingers
to touch things.

When I see a cat I use my sense of sight. When
I hear music I use my sense of hearing. When I smell
food I use my sense of smell. When I suck a sweet
I use my sense of taste. When I feel a piece of wood
I use my sense of touch.

My senses give information to my brain.

This pictogram shows children's shoe sizes. ➡️

Class 5. Size of our shoes.

Number of children (7, 6, 5, 4, 3, 2, 1)

Size of shoes: 9 10 11 12 13 1 2 3

1 How many wear size 2 shoes?

2 Which size is worn most?

3 What is the smallest shoe size in the class?

4 Guess how many children in your class wear the same size shoes as you. Write down your guess.

5 Find out the shoe sizes of all the children in your class.

6 Make a **pictogram** to show these sizes.

7 How many children wear the same size shoes as you?

8 Was your guess right?

9 Which size is worn most in your class?

A plan

This is Krisha's classroom.

Key:

▭	children's table
▭	teacher's desk
▫	chair
▨	bookcase
○	bin
⊟	sink
▬	blackboard
〰	store
▦	bench
◿	door

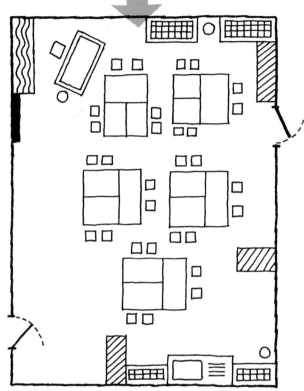

1 Use the **key** to help you finish this chart.

	Item	How many in classroom
⊟	sink	1
▦	bench	4
▭	children's table	
▭	teacher's desk	
▫		

2 Draw a plan of your classroom or a room in your home. Make a key for your plan.
Use colours if you wish.

Book titles

You can learn a lot about a book just by reading its **title**.

Search the book titles on page 13 to help you answer these questions.

1 Which book might tell you how to feed a goldfish?

2 Which book might tell you about grey squirrels?

3 Which two books might help you to learn about robins?

4 Which two books would you use to find out about ponies?

5 Which three books would be useful for a dog owner?

6 Which of the books would you choose for yourself? Write a reason for your choice.

7 Draw two shapes like this:

In one shape write the titles of two books about wild animals. In the other shape write the titles of two books about animals which are not wild.

8 Draw an interesting front cover for a book about your favourite animal. Don't forget to write a title on your cover.

Book titles

Alphabetical order

a b c d e f g h i j k l m n o p q r s t u v w x y z

1 Choose and write the letter from each box which comes first in the alphabet. You will find a hidden message.

| z y | o t | u v | | d a | r w | f e | | s r | i k | j g | h m | x t |

In a dictionary words are in alphabetical order.

cat comes before **d**og . Its first letter **c** comes before the **d** of dog in the alphabet.

2 Write each pair of these words in alphabetical order. The **first letter** of each word helps you.

baby, child	toy, dog	mouse, hen
live, road	friend, park	street, game

3 Now write all twelve words in alphabetical order. Write them in a **list**.

4 Try to learn the first half of the alphabet from **a** to **m** .

5 Ask a friend to test you.

An animal

Carefully read this:

This animal lives in Britain. It looks like a dog.
Its fur is reddish brown.

1 Write which animal you think it is.

It has pointed ears and a bushy tail. It lives in
a hole in the ground called an earth. The mother fox is
called a vixen. She has three to six cubs in a litter.

2 Did you write the right animal?

3 What is the right animal?

4 Write the sentence which proves it.

5 **Search** to find:
The name of the home of the animal.
The name given to the mother of the animal.
The name of the young of the animal.

6 **Search** the titles of real books to help you find
a book which has a picture of this animal.
Use it to help you draw the animal and
write a sentence about it.

The garden spider's web

Search page 17 to find out.

1 How does the spider start its web?

2 What is the web made from?

3 How many spirals does the spider make?

4 Why does the spider need the dry spiral?

5 Why is the second spiral sticky?

6 What sort of spider makes a web this way?

7 Why do spiders make webs?

8 Look at page 17 to help you draw a spider's web.

Next time you see a spider's web look at it closely. Make a drawing of what you see.

The garden spider's web

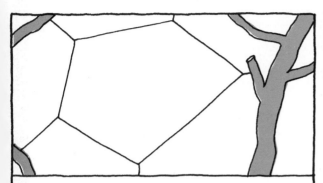

1 First the spider makes a frame from silk.

2 Next the spider goes across the frame. It makes the first spoke.

3 The spider spins more silk thread. It fixes all the spokes.

4 The spider makes a spiral from the centre to the frame. It uses dry thread.

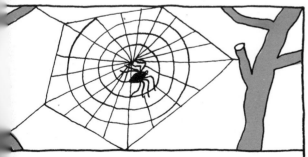

5 The spider walks on the dry spiral and spins another spiral. This is sticky.

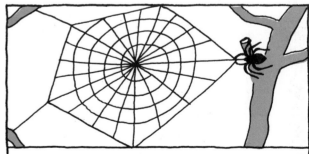

6 As the spider spins the sticky spiral it takes away the dry spiral. Then it waits to catch some food in the web.

Grey squirrels

Search page 19 and use the **headings** to help you write the correct information.

1 Grey squirrels come from:

> Choose the correct word to finish the sentence. → Canada
> → America
> → Scotland

2 Grey squirrels live in: trees
hedges
holes

3 The fur on their backs is mainly: red
brown
greyish

4 They also have fur which is: yellow
white
pink

5 How long is the grey squirrel from its nose to the tip of its tail?

6 How do grey squirrels store food?

7 Write two things that squirrels eat.

8 What do you think makes squirrels very good at climbing and jumping?

Grey squirrels

The grey squirrel

Grey squirrels live in many parts of Britain. They were brought from North America. They have greyish fur on their backs. They have white fur underneath. The length of the head and body is about 28 centimetres. The length of the tail is about 21 centimetres.

The squirrel's home

Squirrels build their homes in trees. The homes are called dreys. They are made from twigs and leaves. Squirrels spend a lot of time in trees. They are very good at climbing and jumping.

The squirrel's food

Squirrels eat acorns, nuts and fir cone seeds. They often bury food for the winter.

How to draw a squirrel

The sentences on page 21 are mixed up.
They should tell you how to draw a squirrel.

1 Write the sentences in the proper order.
These drawings will help you.

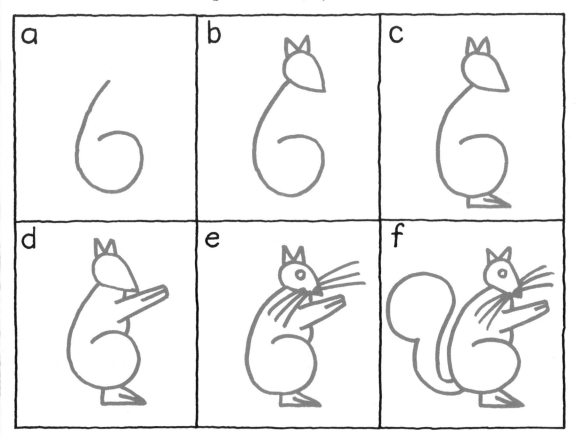

2 Draw the squirrel.

How to draw a squirrel

Draw a lovely bushy tail.

Draw the legs at the bottom.

Draw the eyes, nose and whiskers.

Draw a large number six like this 6

Draw the head and ears.

Draw the front and the front legs.

21

Alphabetical order

a b c d e f g h i j k l m n o p q r s t u v w x y z

1 Write each set of letters in **alphabetical order**.

| d, a, b, c, e | h, j, k, i, g, f | p, o, n, m, l |

| q, u, s, t, r | x, z, w, y, v |

2 Write each set of words in alphabetical order.
The **first letter** of each word helps you.

dog, cat, pig, horse

fur, claw, paw, beak

nest, den, stable, cage

3 Choose three of the words you have written.
Find them in a dictionary.
Write what it says about them
using your own words.

4 Try to learn the
second half of the
alphabet from n to z .
Ask a friend
to test you.

22

A map

This is the map of a town centre:

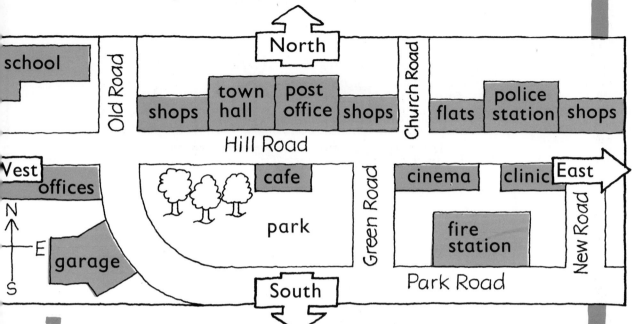

1 In which road is:
the school? the post office?
the fire station?

North, east, south and west are written on the
sides of the map. Use these words to help you.

2 Name three buildings on the north side of Hill Road.

3 Name three buildings on the south side of Hill Road.

4 Name three roads which are east of the post office.

5 Name three buildings which are west of the cinema.

6 Find a map of the area around your school.
Use it to help you draw the roads near your
school. Write **north**, **east**, **south** and **west** on
the sides of the map you have drawn.

23

Letters

1 Draw each of these pictures. Leave a space for writing under each one.

2 **Search** page 25 to help you write a sentence to go with each picture.

3 **Search** book titles to help you find a book about stamps. Use it to help you write one or two interesting things about stamps.

Letters

When you have written a letter you put it in an envelope. You write the address carefully and stick on a stamp. You post the letter in a post box.

A postman or postwoman will empty the post box. The letters will be taken to a sorting office. There the letters are sorted by fast machines and put into mail bags. Many mail bags are carried on trains to other towns. Some letters are taken by ship or plane to places far away.

The letters are carefully sorted again by another postman or postwoman. The letters are then delivered to the right address.

Firefighters

Search page 27 to find out.

1 What is used to put out most fires?

2 Why do firefighters wear helmets? Write two reasons.

3 When is breathing gear used?

4 What does the fire engine pump do?

5 What tool is the firefighter holding?

6 Why is the tool needed?

7 What letter is on the roadside sign?

8 What does the letter stand for?

9 Search the titles of real books to help you find some books about firefighters. Use them to write one or two interesting things about fighting fires.

10 Would you like to work at a fire station? Write a reason for your answer.

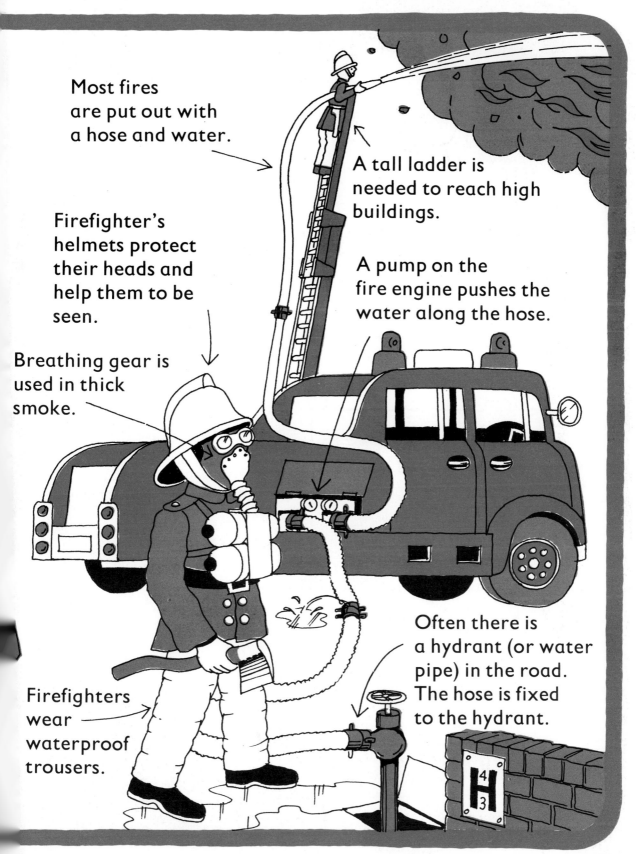

Most fires
are put out with
a hose and water.

A tall ladder is
needed to reach high
buildings.

Firefighter's
helmets protect
their heads and
help them to be
seen.

A pump on the
fire engine pushes the
water along the hose.

Breathing gear is
used in thick
smoke.

Often there is
a hydrant (or water
pipe) in the road.
The hose is fixed
to the hydrant.

Firefighters
wear
waterproof
trousers.

H
4
3

Policewomen and policemen

Search page 29
for help with **1, 2** and **3**.

1 Write two ways in which the police help us.

2 Why do the police often wear a uniform?

3 Make a drawing of three things the police carry.
Write a sentence to go with each drawing.

4 Search book titles to help you find books about the police.
Use the books to help you write two interesting things about the police.

5 Would you like to be a policewoman or policeman?
Write a reason for your answer.

Policewomen and policemen

Policewomen and policemen are very useful to us.
They help us when we are lost. They look after us when
there is danger on the roads. They try to make sure that
everyone obeys the law.

It is easy to see policewomen or policemen on duty.
They wear dark blue uniforms.

The police often carry these useful things:
1 a note book to write in;
2 a card to prove they are policemen or policewomen;
3 a small radio to speak to the police station;
4 a whistle to blow if they need help;
5 a torch to see in the dark;
6 handcuffs to use when they arrest somebody.

A block chart

This shows where children in a class would choose to work.

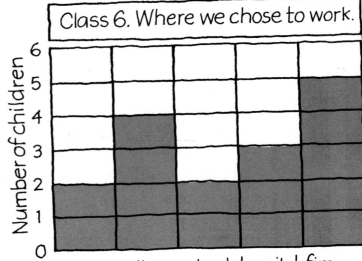

Class 6. Where we chose to work.

Number of children (vertical axis: 0 to 6)

post office, police station, school, hospital, fire station (horizontal axis)

1 Which place did **most** children choose?

2 Which two places did **fewest** choose?

3 Guess which of the places most of your friends would choose to work. Write down your guess.

4 Make a chart like this:

Post office	
Police station	
School	
Hospital	
Fire station	

Put the ticks here.

5 Ask about fifteen children. Tick their choice on the chart.

6 Make a block chart to show the information. Use squared paper.

7 Was your guess  right?
nearly right?
wrong?

Alphabetical order

a b c d e f g h i j k l m n o p q r s t u v w x y z

1 Write each set of words in **alphabetical order**.
The first letter of each word helps you.

> **c**halk, **a**xe, **n**otebook, **l**etter

> teacher, firefighter, nurse, doctor

> school, office, hospital, factory

2 In the groups of words below, the first letters are
the same. Use the **second letter** of each word
to help you write each group in alphabetical order.

> fire, fat, flame

> book, ball, beads, birthday

> stamp, sack, ship, sort

3 Choose three of the words you have written. Find
them in a dictionary. Write what it says about
them, using your own words.

4 Check that you know the
whole alphabet. Ask a friend
to test you.

Notes for the teacher

This Study Skills course aims to develop the study skills of readers in primary education. Specific chronological or reading ages are not quoted for the four levels as these are just two factors to be considered when matching the course to the child. The teacher will need to ensure that the child can proceed with **confidence, understanding** and reasonable **independence**.

The course provides a wide range of **skill-building experiences** which contribute towards the development of a **strategy for study**:

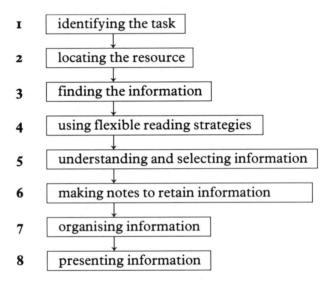

1   identifying the task

2   locating the resource

3   finding the information

4   using flexible reading strategies

5   understanding and selecting information

6   making notes to retain information

7   organising information

8   presenting information

Assignments at each level are grouped into three themes:

Level 1	self, family, friends	animals	people at work
Level 2	buildings	trees	transport
Level 3	food	communication	explorers
Level 4	problems and solutions	inventions and discoveries	the solar system